DANGER ZONE:
Dieting and Eating Disorders™

ANOREXIA

Stephanie Watson

ROSEN
PUBLISHING®

New York

Published in 2007 by The Rosen Publishing Group, Inc.
29 East 21st Street, New York, NY 10010

Library of Congress Cataloging-in-Publication Data

Watson, Stephanie.
Anorexia / Stephanie Watson.—1st ed.
    p. cm.—(Danger zone: dieting and eating disorders)
Includes bibliographical references.
ISBN-13: 978-1-4042-1996-0
ISBN-10: 1-4042-1996-X
1. Anorexia nervosa—Juvenile literature. I. Title.
RC552.A5W38 2007
616.85'262—dc22

                                            2006033286

Manufactured in the United States of America

Contents

1

What Is Anorexia Nervosa?

Anorexia nervosa, commonly called anorexia, is a deadly illness. But unlike the flu or a sexually transmitted disease (STD), anorexia isn't spread by bacteria or a virus. Instead, anorexia stems from your thoughts and emotions.

Currently, more than eight million Americans suffer from eating disorders. Ninety to 95 percent of those who suffer are female, and the number of males with eating disorders is increasing. There are many men and adolescent males who go undiagnosed either because of the lack of reporting the disorder or because of misdiagnoses. According to H. W. Hoek and D. van Hoeken's article in *International Journal of Eating Disorders* (2003), 40 percent of the newly diagnosed cases of anorexia are girls and young women who are between the ages of fifteen and nineteen.

Although statistics show more female than male sufferers, both young men and young women grapple with eating disorders.

Doctors are slowly beginning to better understand anorexia. There are now treatments that can help people who have anorexia gain self-esteem and get healthy.

ABOUT ANOREXIA NERVOSA

You may have heard the term "anorexia" used before—maybe you talked about it in health class, read about it in a magazine, or heard someone talk about how actress Mary-Kate Olsen was being treated for it. Your mom may get upset if you don't want to finish your dinner and say, "Please eat! You haven't been eating enough food lately. You've lost some weight already—are you still concerned about losing more weight? You aren't becoming ill are you?"

Chances are, eating-related issues probably influence your life or that of a family member or friend right now. You, he, or she might already feel a few of the forces that cause an eating disorder to kick in: insecurity, peer pressure, and society's pressure to be thin.

In spite of fame and fortune, some celebrities, like Mary-Kate Olsen, struggle with eating disorders.

What Is Anorexia Nervosa?

The word "anorexia" literally means "loss of appetite." But anorexia is more like self-starvation—becoming so obsessed with losing weight and dieting that you ignore your body's hunger signals. Although people with anorexia are always hungry, they take pride in denying hunger, feeling more in control and independent. This belief has very dangerous consequences. If anorexia progresses far enough, you can lose massive amounts of body weight—enough to cause psychological problems, physical problems, and even death.

EATING DISORDERS

How do you feel about food? You probably don't have a simple answer.

You need food in order to survive and grow. But eating also has emotional and social importance for everyone. It's how people bond with each other on holidays, at the movies, and at home. And sometimes there are expectations, even pressures about what and how much you eat.

If you have a healthy relationship with food, you're able to eat when you are hungry and enjoy what you eat. If you don't have a healthy relationship with food, eating can cause discomfort, guilt, conflicts with others, and even self-hatred.

An eating disorder usually arises when other influences, such as low self-esteem, abuse in the home, or peer pressure, contribute to the food becoming an avenue to control something in a person's life or a symptom of other things that might be happening in a person's life. These negative feelings about food become overwhelming enough to interfere with your health and nutrition. Your eating becomes "disordered," causing both physical and emotional troubles.

CATEGORIES OF ANOREXIA

People who have anorexia do one or both of these things:

- Restrict the amount of food they eat, and/or exercise all the time to keep their weight down. Someone with anorexia might eat only a tiny portion of food and then jog in place for thirty minutes to work off the calories.

- Eat a lot of food at once (called bingeing) and then get rid of the food by vomiting, taking laxatives or diuretics (such as drugs that reduce fluids), or using enemas (called purging) regularly. This bingeing and purging behavior resembles bulimia nervosa, an eating disorder in which binge eating is followed by purging, fasting, or excessive exercise. Many bulimics are usually preoccupied with the fear of gaining weight. People with anorexia usually refuse to eat, whereas people with bulimia usually binge eat but then purge. Anorexics also usually deny to themselves and to others that there is a problem. Bulimics are often aware that there is a problem, but they may try to keep it a secret from others.

WHO GETS ANOREXIA?

Anyone can get anorexia—male or female, young or old, and from all walks of life. However, anorexia is much more common in teens than in adults. It seldom sets in after age twenty-five. There is also a higher rate of anorexia among females than among males. This may be because society puts much more pressure on young women than on young men to be thin. Also, since anorexia is thought of mainly as a woman's problem, men may be too shy to seek help, so they may be underrepresented in the statistics.

Because not all people with an eating disorder seek help, no one is sure exactly how many people suffer from anorexia. But the U.S. National Library of Medicine indicated in 2004 that it's estimated that 1 to 2 out of every 100 women have struggled with anorexia at some time in

Young women feel a lot of societal pressure to be thin. This pressure can be fueled by movies, magazines, and the fashion and entertainment industries.

their lives. The numbers may even be as high as 10 out of every 100 adolescent girls, according to the Mayo Clinic in 2006. The National Association of Anorexia Nervosa and Associated Disorders (ANAD) reported that young women with anorexia are twelve times more likely to die than women who don't have anorexia—the highest death rate of any emotional problem. Anorexia is much less common in boys and men than in girls and women. Only 1 or 2 out of every 1,000 males have anorexia.

You could become anorexic if you tend to have very low self-esteem or if you are frequently a high achiever. Many people use anorexia as a way to gain more control over their lives. If you feel that your parents or teachers get to make all your decisions for you, you may start to restrict the amount of food you eat to gain control at least over that part of your life.

ANOREXIA: THE BASICS

You may have anorexia if any of these statements apply to you:

- You weigh 15 percent less than the normal body weight for your height and age. For example, if your doctor says you should weigh 100 pounds (45.4 kilograms) and you weigh only 85 pounds (38.6 kg), you're 15 percent below your normal body weight. It's not anorexia if you have a health problem that is causing you to lose weight, though, because that's weight loss you can't control. But if you are trying to keep your weight low on purpose—that is, if you refuse to gain weight—you may have anorexia.
- You're very afraid of gaining weight, even if you aren't overweight. If you obsess about every bite of food that you put in your mouth, worrying that it has too many calories, you may have anorexia. That fear can begin to control you to the point where you think about avoiding food all the time.

- You don't like what you see in the mirror. Even though everyone tells you that you're thin, you see a fat person staring back at you.
- You have amenorrhea, the absence of menstruation by the age of sixteen or so or where the menstrual cycle has stopped for about six months or for the time of about three menstrual periods.

ANOREXIA AND THE BODY

Anorexia can have a big effect on your body and mind. If you have anorexia, you are afraid of getting fat, so you avoid eating. The result is weight loss. At first, the drop in weight may not be noticeable or look unhealthy. But in a short time, the weight loss becomes dramatic and threatens your health.

Anorexia affects all of your body functions. As the disorder progresses, your digestion slows down and you become constipated. Later, during the progression, you're always cold because you've lost the protective layer of fat that insulates you. Fine hair, called lanugo, grows all over your body. If you're female, your menstrual period stops. You also will look and feel tired and weak, have a pasty complexion, lose your hair, and have fainting spells and headaches. The soles of your palms and feet turn yellow because your body is lacking many of the nutrients it needs to function properly. Some of these side effects may not occur until severe weight loss has occurred.

When you aren't getting enough nutrition from food, your body will start to break down muscles in order to produce energy. Your liver and kidneys are damaged from this stress, leading to kidney failure. This can be fatal, or require you to be on dialysis for the rest of your life.

Anorexia may make females infertile, or unable to have children, because fertility depends on having a certain amount of body fat. You may also develop osteoporosis— a condition in which your bones become brittle and may even break. Low bone mineral density in adolescent women who suffer from anorexia is a common problem, partly because of low calcium intake. Even young women who take calcium in their food or in supplements can get osteoporosis because amenorrhea can prevent their bodies from totally absorbing the calcium.

Your heart can be especially affected. Anorexia disturbs the mineral balance in your body, which can cause cardiac arrest and death.

ANOREXIA AND EMOTIONS

Anorexia often begins because of emotional reasons. People who suffer from eating disorders are trying to use food as a way to fill emotional needs, such as love and belonging, to ease loneliness, or to avoid difficult feelings and/or memories.

Yet anorexia actually worsens a painful emotional cycle. You become stressed out when you're around food because you feel tempted to eat. And if you do eat, you feel defeat and regret—you may even hate yourself. These feelings become so overwhelming, it's common for depression to set in.

Anorexia makes it hard for you to think and perceive things normally. When your body isn't getting the nutrients it needs, you run on adrenaline (a hormone that kicks in when you're fearful or stressed) instead of on energy from food. These chemical changes affect your personality. You have wider mood swings and a quicker temper.

Also, the more weight you lose, the more distorted your body image becomes. You see fat on your body when you really are dangerously thin. Thought distortion occurs because of the lack of nutrients. You also might not be able to concentrate.

OTHER EATING DISORDERS

If you have anorexia, you might have had a bout with another eating disorder, although this should not be assumed.

Besides anorexia, the most common eating disorders are bulimia nervosa and compulsive eating (also called binge eating disorder). Experts estimate that almost 50 percent of people with anorexia have also struggled with another eating disorder at some time.

BULIMIA NERVOSA

People who suffer from bulimia nervosa, or bulimia, binge (eat a large quantity of food in a short time) and then purge (eliminate the food, usually by vomiting, using laxatives, or taking diuretics, also known as water pills). Bulimia also does major damage to the body.

Anorexia can lead to chemical imbalances, which can affect your mood and mental health, as well as your physical health.

Myths and Facts About Anorexia Nervosa

Myth: The only people who get anorexia are young white women.

Fact: People of all ages, genders, and races can get anorexia.

Myth: You can tell whether someone has anorexia by how skinny they are.

Fact: To be diagnosed with anorexia, a person needs to be 15 percent under his or her average body weight. Only severe anorexics are very underweight.

Myth: All body changes that result from anorexia are reversible.

Fact: Anorexia can damage organs such as the heart, liver, and kidneys permanently.

Myth: Anorexia allows you to have more control over your life.

Fact: Anorexia can actually make you become more out of control, because it causes uncontrollable changes to your body and personality.

Myth: It's risky to admit that you have anorexia because people will think you're crazy.

Fact: Asking for help is the best thing that you can do when you have anorexia. If you find an adult you can trust, he or she can get you the help you need to become healthy again.

It can cause ulcers (holes or tears) in the stomach, throat, and mouth. People with bulimia can develop yellow, damaged teeth from the acids brought up into the mouth through repeated vomiting. Abusing laxatives causes painful stomach cramps and weakens the digestive system.

COMPULSIVE EATING

Compulsive eating is a disorder in which a person eats uncontrollably but doesn't purge afterward. People with compulsive eating disorder eat large amounts of food very quickly whether or not they feel hungry. They usually do this in private and feel unable to control how much or what they eat. People who regularly overeat may forget how to read their body's normal hunger signals and may not know how to satisfy them.

OTHER EATING-RELATED PROBLEMS

Having an eating disorder doesn't mean only restricting what you eat. Many eating disorders have different diagnoses from anorexia, based on the other behaviors involved with the eating disorders. Many people with eating disorders exercise compulsively or abuse medicines. Compulsive exercise is an unhealthy drive to overexercise in order to burn calories and stay thin. This may mean running dozens of miles a day or vowing to do twenty situps for every bite of food you take. Compulsive exercise puts stress on your organs and joints, causing stress fractures and torn muscles.

People with eating-related problems may also abuse medicines and drugs. This includes taking appetite suppressants (drugs that speed up your metabolism), diuretics (drugs that make your body lose water through frequent urination), laxatives (drugs that bring on a bowel movement), and drugs to induce vomiting.

What Is Anorexia Nervosa?

By forcing food and water out of your body, you are upsetting your body's normal functions. Abusing laxatives can cause you to lose control over your bowels. When you stop using laxatives, your body becomes swollen from retaining water. Other over-the-counter diet drugs can help bring on mineral imbalances that lead to heart failure.

What Causes Anorexia Nervosa?

Think of anorexia as a forest fire. You need to have all the right conditions for it to start. But if the conditions are right, all it needs is one spark to set it off. And once it starts, it has the potential to spread fast and out of control if it is not caught in time.

Anorexia can be sparked in many ways. For example, it can start as a diet—a resolution to shed five or ten pounds—that soon gets out of control.

The amount of stress in your life can play a role in the onset of anorexia. Anorexia is more likely to set in during a time of crisis or transition, such as reaching puberty, going to a new school, breaking up with someone, or having family problems.

There are many other factors that help set the stage for anorexia, too. It's important to know as much as you can about how eating disorders take hold so you can keep yourself from falling into dangerous patterns.

THE MIND AND ANOREXIA

The mind is a powerful tool. Without it, you could not think, feel emotions, or do just about anything else. But sometimes, the mind can cause you to do harm to your own body.

People who have anorexia tend to have similar thoughts or emotions that put them at risk for an eating disorder. You may have low self-esteem and low self-worth. You may be obsessive or compulsive, focusing on one thing in your life over and over again. Or, you may have an unnatural desire to be perfect.

YOUR EMOTIONS

Anorexia has a lot to do with your emotions. Often, it sets in when you can't put your feelings into words or openly handle what's bothering you. With anorexia, losing weight becomes an obsession—a very intense, persistent thought that you can't block out.

You may be very afraid that you are fat or are getting fat. At the same time, you may want to stifle these feelings. This leads to an increased desire for control over your emotions and actions.

CONTROL

Often, people with anorexia will view not eating or compulsive exercising as solutions to problems, vowing to lose another 5 pounds (2.3 kg) when they feel upset or stressed out. They try to control their bodies by denying food when they can't control what is happening around them.

This is especially true if many things in your life feel beyond your control. If you aren't allowed to make decisions for yourself or have suffered physical, verbal, or sexual abuse, you may turn to dieting and exercise as ways to find control in your life.

Using anorexia as a way to find control quickly becomes self-destructive. As anorexia sets in, it starts to control you. Soon all of your thoughts and actions revolve around food and eating rather than the emotions you are feeling.

If you feel out of control in your life, it is important to ask for help. Sometimes that just means telling people how you feel. For example, if your parents make family decisions without asking your opinion, you can tell them that you

If you suffer from anorexia, food can feel like your enemy.

want to be more involved. Then
you can work on a plan to keep you
in the decision-making loop.

However, if you are in an abusive situation, you need
to take strong action. Tell an adult you trust that you need
help. A teacher, guidance counselor, relative, or the parent
of a friend can help you find a way to be safe.

THE BODY AND ANOREXIA

Your emotions and your desire to have more control over
your life can play big roles in whether you develop anorexia.
But sometimes it's not your mind, but your body, that causes
an eating disorder.

You may have a mother or sister who had anorexia, and
it runs in your family, partly because of learned behavior,

eating patterns, and a possible genetic factor that might increase the risk of developing anorexia (for example, some researchers believe that certain inherited neurotic symptoms such as anxiety or depression can contribute to this risk). Or, your family may be obsessed with being perfect. Some scientists believe that anorexia might also stem from chemicals in the brain. However, anorexia may not be passed along to family members, too.

GENETIC LINK

Although anorexia is usually thought to be related to emotions and social pressures, doctors are beginning to believe

Researchers are exploring the possibility of a genetic basis to anorexia.

that some people may have genes (traits inherited from your mother and father) that predispose them to having anorexia. These genes cause their brain to tell them not to eat. However, this genetic link has not been confirmed yet. A Dutch team of researchers at Utrecht University who were involved in eating disorder studies in 2001 are currently examining a mutation in a gene coding for a protein that is vital in regulating food intake. The researchers found that the mutation occurred in 11 percent of the 145 anorexic patients they were studying. Though they believe there is a genetic component to the risk of developing anorexia, they do not think that there is a single gene that is involved in the disorder.

Because of a possible genetic link, anorexia tends to run in families. If your sister or mother has anorexia, you could get it, too. But even if you have a genetic risk of developing the disorder or a family history, it doesn't mean you will definitely get anorexia.

THE PERFECT FAMILY

Does your mom constantly complain that she's too fat? Is your older sister always on a diet? Having family members who are obsessed with their weight could rub off on you.

It's not only the urge to diet that tends to run in families. Your sister may be a gymnast and practice five hours every day. Your father might be a workaholic who spends eighty hours per week in the office. Perfectionism and other compulsions are traits that can make it easier for you to develop anorexia. These traits could be in your family's genes, or you could develop them from watching your family.

CHEMICALS IN THE BODY

Often, people with eating disorders have imbalances of hormones and other chemicals in their body. Not eating enough of the right foods could cause these imbalances, but it's also possible that the chemicals themselves help trigger the eating disorder if other factors are there or if the environmental background sets the stage for it.

People with anorexia tend to have high levels of the hormone cortisol, which gets the body ready to react to a stressful situation. Part of this hormone's job is to inhibit a chemical called neuropeptide Y, which stimulates appetite. Scientists think cortisol might help explain why people with anorexia respond to stressful situations by limiting their food.

The brain chemical serotonin may also have something to do with anorexia. This chemical gives you a feeling of well-being and affects your appetite. Researchers have found that people with anorexia have different levels of serotonin than people who don't have anorexia. They have found that people who become anorexic have too much serotonin, then they starve themselves, which lowers the serotonin, but then the brain adapts to the change by adding more serotonin to the body. It becomes a vicious circle because the little bit of serotonin sets off the brain receptors, and the receptors keep trying to adjust.

SOCIETY'S IMPACT

Our society places a high value on thinness. In fact, many people believe that in order to be beautiful, you have to be thin.

When the media—television, movies, and advertising—widely promote this ideal, it becomes difficult to ignore. And it affects what you think is normal. You may start to think that all people are supposed to look as thin as actors and models, when in fact very few people in the world are that thin.

This ideal also affects your feelings about yourself. You may think that losing weight will make you feel more beautiful, loved, accepted, or popular. But trying to be that thin is unhealthy and impossible for most people.

THIN WASN'T ALWAYS IN

Even though thin is popular now, that wasn't always the case. From thousands of years ago up to the mid-1960s, the ideal woman was shapely and soft. Women with full figures were considered desirable because they represented fertility, sexuality, and wealth.

You can see this ideal in the art of many societies. Often, goddesses were portrayed with curvy breasts, stomachs, and buttocks. You also can see this ideal of the female body in the Renaissance paintings of Peter Paul Rubens (this is why full-figured women sometimes are called Rubenesque).

This ideal of the female body held true for a long time. But somewhere along the way, ideas changed. And they have had dramatic effects on American society even very recently.

For example, during the 1950s and 1960s, actress Marilyn Monroe was one of America's most popular sex symbols. She had a beautiful, voluptuous body. But did you know that if Marilyn were modeling today, she would wear a size 16? That size is hard to find in today's most popular stores, much less on women in television, movies, modeling, or advertising!

What Causes Anorexia Nervosa?

The thin-ideal went to the extreme by the end of the twentieth century. In the 1990s, the "heroin chic" look (characterized by a pale complexion and a drug-addict/wasted-away appearance) became popular. Models in the fashion industry (both male and female) with very thin bodies and dark circles under their eyes became the ultimate statement of what was cool and sexy.

Although the "heroin chic" look has mainly gone out of fashion, thin is definitely still in, and the thinner the better. Hosts on the red carpet at the Academy Awards ceremony praise actresses for looking especially skinny. Celebrities brag about how quickly they were able to get back into their "size 0 jeans" after having a baby. You may

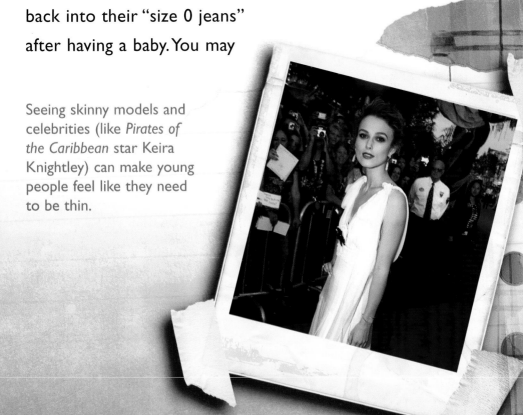

Seeing skinny models and celebrities (like *Pirates of the Caribbean* star Keira Knightley) can make young people feel like they need to be thin.

see those messages and feel like you have to be that thin yourself.

WHAT'S WRONG WITH THIN BEING IN?

Placing too much value on thinness has had negative consequences, especially for teenage girls. It can lead you to become anti-fat—cutting all fat out of your diet and trying to eliminate it from your body. And that can lead to unhealthy dieting and anorexia, which interrupt how you're supposed to grow.

People need to eat healthy foods to take care of their bodies. And as a teen, you need to eat even more than other people because your body is still growing and changing.

Another problem with wanting to be thin is that most people are not naturally thin. All bodies look different and grow at different rates. Genes (the traits inherited from your mother and father) play a major role in deciding what body shape you will have, just as they determine the color of your hair and your eyes.

Some U.S. medical researchers believe that culture or heritage is one of the causes leading to eating disorders in American society. For example, they suggest that some cultural origins, such as Catholic, Jewish, or Italian, might lead to a higher risk of developing an eating disorder because of cultural attitudes about the importance of the role of food in their lives. Other researchers have found that some Hispanic or Asian-American adolescent girls may have higher numbers of eating disorders because they display greater discontent with their bodies.

If you have set an unrealistic goal about how you want to look, you will feel disappointed when you cannot attain it. This can cause the depression that contributes to the onset of eating disorders.

MESSAGES FROM FRIENDS AND FAMILY

Having friends is important. You want to fit in and be accepted. But fitting in can mean feeling pressure to dress, look, and act in a way that reinforces the problems that lead to eating disorders. Many people—girls especially—will bond through "fat talk," or sympathizing over how fat they think they look and how much they hate their bodies. As a group, you may be bringing each other down.

Like your friends, family members may indulge in fat talk. It isn't uncommon for parents and kids to go on diets together—even when the son or daughter hasn't hit puberty yet.

Sometimes parents may directly criticize you for what you look like or how much you eat. This may be intended

Acceptance and support from your friends can help you keep a healthy attitude toward food and weight. Try to keep discussions about weight and appearance positive.

as concern for your social life and goals—"If you keep eating desserts every night, you'll never find a prom date." But it does more harm than good. The message comes across that you're not good enough the way you are.

These kinds of negative comments can set up a battlefield mentality between you and your parents. By commenting on your food intake, your parents come across as criticizing—even controlling—you. And you may respond by defying them.

You may purposely overeat in order to enrage your thin-conscious parents. Or you could fall into anorexic patterns, thinking that being thinner will bring approval or that starvation will bring attention. But these are unhealthy ways to cope with the problem.

It's possible to speak up against the anti-fat mentality. When you want to be accepted by others, it may be hard to believe that weight does not matter. But there are things that matter more—like finding out who you are inside, setting and meeting goals, and tapping into the energy inside of you. If people around you make a big deal about weight, you don't have to go along with it.

Your attitudes about yourself can bring on or prevent an eating disorder. By improving your self-esteem, you can take a giant step toward preventing anorexia.

3

Am I at Risk?

What makes someone likely to develop an eating disorder? There is no single cause. Eating disorders are complex problems. They can be fueled by a combination of things, including society's messages, biological and psychological issues, and family issues. Experts study these factors all the time.

Even if you experience problems in one or more of these areas, it doesn't mean that you automatically will have an eating disorder. But it's important to know whether you have some of these risk factors in your life, so you can stop a potential eating problem before it starts.

RISK FACTORS FOR ANOREXIA

Anorexia has many possible causes. Some of these causes are internal. You may not have high self-esteem, or you may push yourself too hard.

Other causes are external. You may feel pressure from your friends, family, and society to be thin. Or, you may have a really dramatic life change that makes you feel out of control and causes you to start unhealthy eating habits. You may have a genetic predisposition to anorexia, or you may have an abusive or out-of-control family situation that influences your thinking and actions.

SELF-ESTEEM ISSUES

People who have high self-esteem—a positive view of themselves—have less risk of developing an eating disorder. This means that they value their own ideas and opinions, are eager to try new things, and speak up when something is bothering them.

In comparison, people at risk for anorexia tend to have a less-than-flattering attitude about themselves. They feel misunderstood, think their ideas aren't important, try very hard to be perfect, and shy away from trying new things because they're afraid to fail.

If you have low self-esteem, you probably feel that you have little control over what happens to you. There are other attitudes that make you vulnerable to anorexia, too. Ask yourself the following questions:

Low self-esteem can play a big role in the development of an eating disorder.

- **Do you minimize your accomplishments?** This means you don't credit yourself where credit is due. If you score the winning point in a basketball game, you say, "Well, anyone could have done it." If you ace a test, you say, "It wasn't that hard anyway." You miss out on enjoying the positive things you're able to achieve, convinced that you still didn't do well enough.
- **Do you not see yourself as others see you?** Other people may see you putting yourself down and tell you that you're better than you give your- self credit for. But you usually discredit what they say by thinking, "Well, she's my mom. Of course she

thinks I'm great" or "He doesn't know what he's talking about."

- **Do you criticize your body?** Any unhappiness and tension that you feel gets directed toward your body. You feel unattractive and imperfect. You think that losing weight will make you feel better about yourself and will make other people like you.

DIETING

Have you ever gone on a diet and lost a few pounds? If you have, you probably have heard comments from your friends and family such as, "Wow, you look great! Did you lose weight?"

Our society values thin, toned bodies. So when someone loses weight, they generally get praised for it, even if they weren't overweight to begin with. Getting cheered on in your weight loss can give you the urge to lose even more weight than you need to lose.

WEIGHT GAIN

If you lose a few pounds, you're likely to hear from friends and family members that you look great. But gain a few pounds, and you may hear just the opposite. Knowing that your weight gain has been noticed and made fun of can really hurt your feelings.

Even worse than getting criticism from the outside is the pressure you feel on the inside. Gaining weight can mean that your body doesn't look exactly the same as it used to look. Maybe your favorite bikini doesn't fit anymore, or you don't look quite as good in your jeans. Intense dieting is one way some people respond to criticism.

LIFE CHANGES

Life is full of uncertainty and change. A move to a new town, parents divorcing, or the death of a family member can all cause major upheavals. These changes can be very emotional and stressful.

One way to cope with the things in your life that you can't control is to try to reign in the things you can control. Eating is one thing in your life that you may believe you can control.

SPORTS AND OTHER ACTIVITIES

The aim in sports is to win. You need to run the fastest, swim the hardest, and score the most goals in order to be the best. With these high expectations, it's no wonder that athletes are at higher risk for eating disorders than other people.

Sports are physically demanding, and people who partici- pate in them need to be in good shape. Some athletes take their quest to be thin too far, though. They think that if they lose more weight, they'll be faster and more agile.

Some sports, like wrestling, actually require that athletes stay within a certain weight range. Others, like figure skating and dancing, press the idea that only thin, lithe bodies look good enough to be on the stage and ice. Parents and coaches can make young athletes even more prone to eating disorders by pushing them to lose weight in order to perform better.

CHANGE IS POSSIBLE

Even if you fit many of the risk factors for anorexia, you are not necessarily destined or doomed to develop an eating disorder. It's possible to overcome many of the risks.

Stay in touch with your feelings and what's going on in your life. Express yourself and don't be afraid to ask for help when you need it. You can use your self-knowledge to keep from falling into the patterns that lead to a full-blown eating disorder. This can mean finding friends who don't make a big deal out of food and body size; writing down your thoughts (taping them on a portable tape recorder works, too); getting involved with sports, hobbies, or youth groups; and/or getting help by talking with a therapist, counselor, or school social worker.

EDUCATE YOURSELF

Know what you're up against. Go to your local library, search the Internet, and talk to your doctor about eating disorders. Know how they start and what they can do to you. Stay away from any sites that promote anorexia. They can encourage you to start making dangerous choices about your health.

Think critically about the advertising you see. If you're sick of magazines showing only waiflike models, let the editors of those magazines know. You can pressure them by saying you won't buy their publications anymore.

BE POSITIVE

Don't go along with fat talk. If your friends are in the habit of putting themselves down and criticizing their bodies, let them know that it bugs you. Be positive. Try saying, "Actually, I like myself. I look just like my aunt did at my age, and I think she's so cool. So what if I'm not a size 2."

Ask your doctor what weight is healthiest for your body. When you see a model in a magazine who is 5'7" and weighs 110 pounds (49.9 kg), you won't have to compare yourself—you'll be able to set your own weight goals.

Get involved with sports that emphasize strength (such as basketball and biking) rather than body shape (such as ballet or gymnastics). Throw out your scale and give away clothes that don't fit. Save up some money to buy clothes that feel comfortable. When you're comfortable and relaxed, your fabulous inner self will shine through. Stop counting calories.

EXPRESS YOUR FEELINGS

Your opinions count. If you're hurt or upset, say so. It's better to disagree with someone than to keep your true feelings inside.

Find an adult you trust (family member, doctor, or counselor) and go to them for help when you start feeling out of control. Always remember that you are not alone. There is help available when and if you need it.

The Quest for Thinness

norexia never happens overnight or for any one reason. If you develop anorexia, you don't necessarily make a conscious choice to put your health and life in jeopardy. Instead, the anorexia is a response to, or way of coping with, the roadblocks to self-esteem and other factors. It gives you something to focus on other than the unhappiness or tension you feel inside. But soon anorexia starts to create its own kind of tension.

IN THE BEGINNING

As you know, anorexia often starts as a diet. But the more weight you lose, the more you want to lose.

In the beginning, you may even receive admiration and praise as you start to lose weight. The attention feels good.

But privately, you feel that you still need to lose more weight. You may exercise for long periods of time to make sure that you keep losing weight and don't level off.

STRICT DIET

One of the first signs of anorexia is that you make your diet regimen more and more strict. This means making what seem to be sensible choices at first—cutting out all red meat, skipping dessert, and choosing low-fat or nonfat alternatives to foods such as cream cheese and salad dressing.

You soon begin restricting your intake of other foods, too. You may limit yourself to white meat and vegetables and reduce the size of your portions. Eventually your diet may become so extreme that you're hardly eating anything.

SELF-PERCEPTION

Soon shedding pounds becomes the most important thing in your life—the yardstick by which you measure and judge yourself. You may start checking yourself in the mirror and weighing yourself several times each day. Your moods are deeply affected by what you see. You're relieved if the scale shows weight loss and devastated if it shows a gain.

Other aspects of your self-perception have changed, too. When you look at your body, you see yourself more as a set of body parts—hips, thighs, stomach—than as a whole person. You become rigid in your thinking, vowing to eliminate pounds in the areas you don't like on your body. You think of losing weight as a positive action, not realizing that this intense scrutiny is actually harming your self-esteem.

THE IMPORTANCE OF RITUALS

Rituals are an important ingredient in the development of anorexia. Often, rituals center around mealtimes. You may devise a rigid plan in which you eat different foods, cut the food up into tiny pieces, and chew a certain number of times before you swallow.

Rigid mealtime routines and rituals can be a danger sign that you are suffering from, or heading toward, anorexia.

It's also common to inspect your food intensely, checking for anything that looks funny. If you find something you can't identify, you feel that it's okay to reject the meal.

SIGNS OF ANOREXIA

As you continue to deny yourself food, your body will begin to change. At first, the changes may not be noticeable to you or people around you. But eventually, the weight loss will have dramatic effects on your looks and physical health.

As you get deeper and deeper into your self-denying rituals, your normal self shuts down even more. Being hungry all the time alters your personality. To a healthy person, your actions will appear more and more irrational.

PERSONALITY CHANGES

One typical change in behavior is that you grow more impatient with others. You become more focused on yourself. You withdraw from friends and family by not going out or returning phone calls. People around you may express serious concern about your extreme weight loss, but you're convinced that they are trying to sabotage you. You feel that the anorexia gives you a sense of power and invincibility.

Although you still believe that the anorexia is making you powerful and in control, you probably feel scared and lonely underneath. This loneliness may become worse as the illness progresses. You may get into more fights with your family, or even worse, watch family members fight about (or over) you. People may start to relate to you differently, alternately babying, arguing with, and avoiding you. You may end up feeling more alienated than you did at the start.

BODY CHANGES

When you have full-blown anorexia, your body will show these physical signs of illness:

- Weight loss of 15 percent below normal weight
- Fatigue or hyperactivity
- Irregular or absent menstrual periods
- Muscle weakness
- Dizziness and/or fainting
- Skin problems
- Feeling cold
- Dizziness or fainting
- Constipation
- Yellow palms and soles
- Loss of hair on your head
- Growth of fine, downy hair (called lanugo) on your body

- Difficulty sleeping
- Bloating
- Dehydration
- Poor circulation
- Cuts on the hands from the teeth during forced vomiting when purging

When you experience these symptoms of anorexia, you are doing major harm to your body.

5

Getting Healthy

Anorexia is not a lifestyle, but it is about making choices. You can choose to starve yourself to the point where you become sick and controlled by your disease, or you can choose to become healthy.

CHOOSING TO STOP

If the anorexia continues, you may risk death. Your organs will start to shut down, and you will have liver, kidney, and heart problems. But it's possible to stop the illness before then. At first, you may not want to stop. Or, you may want to but are afraid to do so. It is scary, but that's part of the illness of anorexia. It makes you feel as if it's the only thing that matters. It makes you fear that if you give up anorexia, you'll be nothing without it—it becomes a part of your identity, so giving it up is a loss, similar to losing a part of yourself.

But the truth is, anorexia is holding you back. It takes up all of your energy—energy you otherwise could spend growing and learning about yourself and living a healthy life.

It is possible to recover with the help of your parents, friends, and doctors. And once you break the pattern, you'll see how quickly new opportunities open to you.

Admitting you have an eating disorder is the hardest thing you can do when you have anorexia. People probably have tried to confront you about it before. But sometimes people's concerns can feel like pressures and threats. They may say, "You're tearing this family apart," or "Your father and I don't know what to do with you," or "If you don't eat something, I'm sending you to a therapist."

You probably want—and need—people's love and concern. It's possible that someone may confront you when the time is right and you're ready to take him or her up on an offer for help. But, especially if you're taken by surprise or someone doesn't express himself or herself in the best way, you're likely to reject any help that is offered.

That's why it's important to take matters into your own hands and choose whom to tell and how to say it. The first time you admit to another person that you have a problem can feel very awkward. But if you think it through first, you'll feel more comfortable when the time comes.

HOW TO GET HELP

Tell an authority figure. You can tell a friend, too, but it's important to tell someone who has more insight about what to do. This could be your parents or a friend's parents, an older sister or brother, a teacher, a counselor, or someone from your religious organization.

Pick a time that's good to talk. Make sure you have enough time and a quiet space. Schedule your meeting in advance, even if it's a family meeting.

Have a support person with you if you need it. This could be a friend or a professional such as a social worker or therapist who already knows that you have an eating disorder.

Think about what you're going to say and how. You don't have to write down a script. But it may help to come up with a few key phrases or points beforehand, such as:

- "I know you have brought this up with me before and I denied it. But I have a problem with food. I'm ready to talk about it now."
- "I haven't been eating. I need your help."

Ten Great Questions to Ask When You're Asking for Help

1. Do I have anorexia?

2. What effects has my anorexia had on my body?

3. What tests will I have to take to check my health?

4. What treatments do I have to choose from?

5. How can I deal with my negative self-image?

6. Can I take medication, and what effects will it have on me?

7. What kind of diet should I be eating?

8. What should I do if I just can't get myself to eat?

9. Should I take nutritional supplements?

10. Is there a healthier way for me to exercise?

- "I need to bring a problem out into the open. I'm afraid of eating. I need to talk with you about what to do."

Be prepared that people's reactions may not be what you expected. Although you have planned in advance, you may find that the person isn't comfortable handling the information. It may mean that someone gets angry at you, tries to one-up you with a story about himself, or goes on as if nothing has happened. If this happens, you will need to speak to another person who can help you.

HOW TO CONFRONT A PERSON WITH ANOREXIA

One of the hardest things you can do is confront someone you think is suffering from anorexia. Here are some tips that may help:

- Educate yourself about the problem. Read up on eating disorders and talk to a therapist or counselor for information.
- Find a quiet time that's good to talk. Don't confront someone when other people are around and an argument could start.
- Use "I" statements instead of "you" statements. Rather than accusing, let the person know gently that

her illness is noticeable and has affected you. For example: "I noticed you haven't been eating. Is something wrong?" This opens up a dialogue more effectively than simply saying, "You look sick."

- Listen to what the person has to say. Hold back comments about yourself and your own problems for the time being.
- Understand that your help may not be taken. It's important to let the person know that you care about her, but if she isn't ready to change, you can't force her.
- Be available if your friend needs to reach out to you in the future.

6

Diagnosing Anorexia and Choosing a Recovery Plan

A good first step if you think you might have anorexia is to visit your primary-care doctor. Even if you haven't been to the doctor in a while, it's important that she knows what's going on.

Your doctor will examine you to see how your eating disorder has affected your health. Often your primary-care physician may refer you to an eating disorder specialist.

First, the doctor will check your overall health: your height and weight, heart rate, blood pressure, temperature, and heartbeat. She will also look for other signs of anorexia, such as brittle nails or dry skin. And she may give you tests that check your heart, chemicals in your blood, and the function of your liver, kidneys, and thyroid gland. Some of these tests will help the doctor know whether your problem is an eating disorder or another health problem.

Then your doctor will probably ask you a few questions, such as:

- How have you been eating?
- How has your weight changed recently?
- What are you doing to lose weight?
- Are you having problems with your family or friends?

CHOOSING THE RIGHT RECOVERY PLAN

To get better, you'll go through one or more different treatments. The treatments can focus on your body and your mind.

It's important to be involved in deciding what your recovery plan will be. Sit down with your primary-care doctor and family and talk about the options that are available. Together, you can decide what works best for you, depending on your needs and your family's financial situation.

THERAPY FOR YOUR BODY

The first goal in your therapy is to get your body healthy. It's possible that if you are very ill, you may need to be hospitalized. The doctors there will monitor your heart and other vital signs, and make sure that you have the right balance of fluids and chemicals in your body.

Because experts have found a connection between eating disorders and depression, antidepressants such as Prozac have been used to treat eating disorders. If you are given a prescription, ask your doctor and therapist about the drug and its side effects. You also have the right to request a change in your medication if you feel it is not working.

Once you're healthy enough to go home, you may see a dietician who specializes in eating disorders. This person can help you plan out your meals to make sure you get enough calories and can help you develop better eating habits.

THERAPY FOR YOUR MIND

One major part of recovery from anorexia is psychotherapy, or therapy for short. This is not as scary as it sounds. Basically, therapy is talking to a neutral person (a therapist) about what's going on in your life. The more you talk, the more you discover about yourself. Sometimes talking can be scary, partly because some people who have anorexia do not feel that they have a voice, or they try to hide that voice. Some experimental therapies, such as music, graphic art, and drama therapies, have proven to be very helpful in the recovery process while treating people with anorexia. People recovering from anorexia can find ways to express their thoughts, opinions, and feelings in nonverbal ways. For example, in music therapy, people can participate in structured groups where they can write songs, beat a drum, and sing karaoke. These interventions have been found to provide ways in which a lack of self-esteem, a fear of rejection, and poor communication skills can be worked on and overcome.

Therapy is especially helpful for dealing with eating disorders. The better you know yourself, the better equipped you are to build your self-esteem. At the same time, you can work on pinpointing the patterns of thought or the life experiences that brought on the eating disorder and prevent them from happening again.

You may find that a clinic situation works best for you. Clinics specializing in eating disorders are often free. They may be inpatient, which means you live there while receiving treatment, or outpatient, which means you come in during the day and go home at night.

These are some of the different kinds of therapy you might try:

- **Individual therapy:** You meet with a therapist one-on-one. A therapist may be a psychologist (a therapist with a Ph.D. degree), a psychiatrist (a psychologist who is also a medical doctor), a licensed professional counselor (LPC), a psychotherapist, or a licensed social worker.
- **Family therapy:** You and your family meet with a therapist. This helps your family learn more about eating disorders and how to help you.

- **Group therapy:** You meet with a group of people who share the same type of problem and, together with a therapist, discuss solutions.
- **Self-help:** You meet with other people who are recovering from eating disorders to share insights. Unlike other avenues to recovery, self-help is not led by a therapist. Members of a group form networks with each other. Self-help also is free.

STAY INVOLVED IN YOUR TREATMENT

No matter what kind of therapy you choose, it's important to stay involved in the decision-making process. That means asking your therapist about her plan for you and how she views the therapy experience.

It's possible that you may be in a treatment plan that isn't working so well for you. Or, you may want to give it all up and go back to anorexic patterns. Don't give up! You already have made the choice for health.

Remember that there are many routes toward recovery. If you can speak up about how you feel, you can work together with others to decide what to do. There are many different approaches for treating anorexia. Sometimes it takes time before you find the right one. Recovery from anorexia is one of the hardest things you will ever do—but it's worth it.

Glossary

adrenaline A hormone that kicks in when you're fearful or stressed.

appetite suppressant A drug or chemical that reduces hunger/appetite and keeps you from wanting as much food.

bingeing Eating large amounts of food in one sitting.

body image The way you perceive your body and how you think others perceive your body.

bulimia An eating disorder in which someone eats a lot and then purges the food.

cardiac arrest When your heart stops beating.

constipation Difficulty having bowel movements.

cortisol A hormone that gets your body ready to deal with stressful situations.

disordered Something that doesn't function in the usual way.

diuretic A drug that causes an increase in the amount of urine the kidneys produce.

enema Placing liquid in the rectum to have a bowel movement.

genes The basic units of heredity.

infertility The inability to have children.

laxative A drug or substance that brings on a bowel movement.

nutrition Eating a healthy selection of foods in the amounts necessary to maintain health.

osteoporosis A condition that causes bones to become fragile.

purge To rid the body of food, usually through vomiting, exercise, or laxatives.

serotonin A chemical in the brain that gives you a feeling of well-being and affects your appetite.

ulcers Tears or holes in the lining of the stomach, throat, or mouth.

Resources

Anorexia Nervosa and Related Eating Disorders, Inc. (ANRED)

www.anred.com

ANRED is a nonprofit group that can teach you more about anorexia and other eating disorders, and help you on the road to recovery.

Helping to End Eating Disorders (HEED)
191 Sweet Hollow Rd.
Old Bethpage, NY 11804

(516) 694-1054

www.helpingendeatingdisorders.org

HEED can help you and your family deal with your eating disorder. It can refer you to people who offer many different kinds of therapy.

National Association of Anorexia Nervosa and
   Associated Disorders (ANAD)

P.O. Box 7

Highland Park, IL 60035

(847) 831-3438

www.anad.org/site/anadweb

ANAD is a resource center that can point you to the best sources and facilities to get treatment.

National Eating Disorders Association (NEDA)

603 Stewart St., Suite 803

Seattle, WA 98101

(800) 931-2237

www.nationaleatingdisorders.org

The NEDA is the biggest nonprofit group in the United States working to prevent eating disorders.

WEB SITES

Due to the changing nature of Internet links, Rosen Publishing has developed an online list of Web sites related to the subject of this book. This site is updated regularly. Please use this link to access the list:

http://www.rosenlinks.com/dz/anor

For Further Reading

Becker, Daniel. *This Mean Disease: Growing Up in the Shadow of My Mother's Anorexia.* Carlsbad, CA: Gürze Books, 2005.

Heffner, Michelle, and Georg H. Eifert. *The Anorexia Workbook: How to Accept Yourself, Heal Your Suffering, and Reclaim Your Life.* Oakland, CA: New Harbinger Publications, Inc., 2004.

Lucas, Alexander R. *Demystifying Anorexia Nervosa: An Optimistic Guide to Understanding and Healing.* New York, NY: Oxford University Press, 2004.

Madaras, Lynda, and Area Madaras. *My Body, My Self for Boys: The 'What's Happening to My Body' Workbook for Boys.* Second ed. New York, NY: Newmarket Press, 2000.

Madaras, Lynda, and Area Madaras. *My Body, My Self for Girls: The 'What's Happening to My Body' Workbook for Girls.* Second ed. New York, NY: Newmarket Press, 2000.

Maisel, Richard, David Epston, and Ali Borden. *Biting the Hand That Starves You: Inspiring Resistance to Anorexia/Bulimia.* New York, NY: W. W. Norton, 2004.

Menzie, Morgan. *Diary of an Anorexic Girl: Based on a True Story.* Nashville, TN: W. Publishing Group, 2003.

Schaefer, Jennifer. *Life Without Ed: How One Woman Declared Independence from Her Eating Disorder and How You Can Too.* New York, NY: McGraw-Hill, 2004.

Smith, Grá Inne. *Anorexia and Bulimia in the Family: One Parent's Practical Guide to Recovery.* New York, NY: Wiley, 2004.

Index

PHOTO CREDITS

Cover, pp. 1, 10, 15 Shutterstock.com; p. 5 (left) www.istockphoto.com/James Pauls; p. 5 (middle) www.istockphoto.com/Gino Santa Maria; p. 5 (right) www.istockphoto.com/Anita Patterson; p. 6 © Peter Kramer/Getty Images; p. 23 © Phanie/Photo Researchers, Inc.; p. 24 www.istockphoto.com/Andrei Tchernov; p. 29 © Kevin Winter/Getty Images; p. 32 www.istockphoto.com/ Nicholas Sutcliffe; p. 36 www.istockphoto.com/Nuno Silva; p. 44 www. istockphoto.com/Sharon Dominick.

Designer: Gene Mollica; Photo Researcher: Amy Feinberg